ACADIA
NATIONAL PARK

by Ruth Radlauer

Photographs
by Ed and Ruth Radlauer

Design and map
by Rolf Zillmer

AN ELK GROVE BOOK

 CHILDRENS PRESS®

CHICAGO

To the naturalists,
who give Acadia National Park
its own special character.

Special thanks to Judy Hazen,
Lois Winter, and Robert Rothe

Photo credits:
 Judy Hazen, pages 31 (top) (bottom),
 33 (Ranger), and 35.

Cover Photo: Lighthouse At Bass Harbor Head

Library of Congress Cataloging in Publication Data

Radlauer, Ruth Shaw.
 Acadia National Park.
 (Parks for people)
 "An Elk Grove book."
 SUMMARY: Presents the geography, plant and animal
life, and distinctive features of this national park on
the coast of Maine.
 1. Acadia National Park—Juvenile literature.
[1. Acadia National Park. 2. National parks and
reserves] I. Radlauer, Edward. II. Title.
F27.M9R3 1978   917.41'45   77-18056
ISBN 0-516-07495-4

4 5 6 7 8 9 10 11 12 13 14 15 R 92 91 90 89 88

Contents

page

What is Acadia National Park? _____ 4

Your Trip to Acadia _____ 6

Map _____ 7

Islands from Mountaintops _____ 8

Soil _____ 10

Gifts from the Soil _____ 12

Mountain Flowers _____ 14

A New Forest _____ 16

Early People _____ 18

Settlers _____ 20

Baker Island _____ 22

Gifts from the Sea — Lobsters _____ 24

Lobstering _____ 26

Gifts from People _____ 28

Making the Most of Your Stay _____ 30

Be a Junior Ranger _____ 32

Discovery Hunts — Creature Features _____ 34

The Tide Pool World _____ 36

Birds _____ 38

Other Animals _____ 40

Mountain Hikes _____ 42

Your Changing Park _____ 44

Other National Parks in the East _____ 46

The Author and Illustrators _____ 48

What Is Acadia National Park?

Acadia National Park is a place of change. Over thousands of years it has changed. And it is still changing from year to year, day to day, and minute to minute.

Even while you visit, Acadia changes. One moment it's a breath of fresh air from a mountaintop that overlooks lakes, bays, and a fjord. Then it's the smell of balsam fir on a wooded trail or the rich, earthy smell of leaf mold on a springy forest floor.

Acadia is changing colors. Sometimes the blue sky is reflected in the water. But both water and sky may change quickly to gray, when islands seem to float on a fog that sneaks in from nowhere.

On shore, pink granite rocks change when ocean waves splash white against them. The rocks turn green, dark red, brown, and white as algae, barnacles, and other sealife cling to their roughness.

Here is an island dotted with lakes and topped with trees. It's being changed every minute by the constant work of weather, wind, and waves. This is your park, the everchanging Acadia National Park.

page 4

Fjords Are Made By Glaciers—Somes Sound

Wooded Trail—Acadia Mountain

Porcupine Islands Seen From Hulls Cove

Pea-Sized Acorn Barnacles

Your Trip to Acadia

Acadia National Park is in the northeast corner of the United States. Most of the park is on Mount Desert Island along with Bar Harbor, Maine, and other towns and villages. Schoodic Peninsula to the east and Isle au Haut about 17 miles to the southwest are outposts of the park.

In the park you can stay as long as 14 days at Seawall or Blackwoods Campgrounds. Campsites have tables, benches, fireplaces, and restrooms nearby. There are no wilderness campsites for overnight backpacking.

You'll want to hike all kinds of trails, so be sure to take hiking shoes or boots, a canteen, and sun hat. Take a sweater and jacket. Your wool cap will keep the cold of summer nights and morning walks from nipping at your ears.

The park is open all year, but most people visit in July and August when more activities are offered. Six months before your trip, write for information to the Superintendent, Acadia National Park, Bar Harbor Maine, 04609. If campground reservations are filled, write to the Chambers of Commerce in Bar Harbor, Northeast Harbor, 04662, and Southwest Harbor, 04679, for information about campgrounds, motels, and cottages.

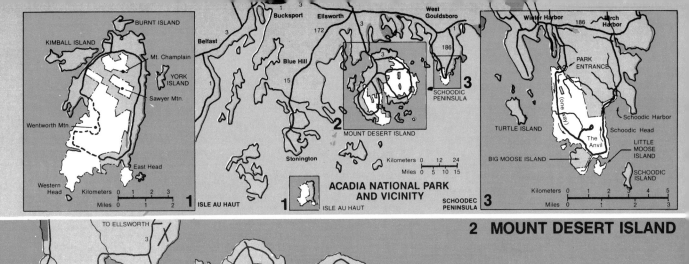

ACADIA NATIONAL PARK AND VICINITY

1 ISLE AU HAUT

3 SCHOODEC PENINSULA

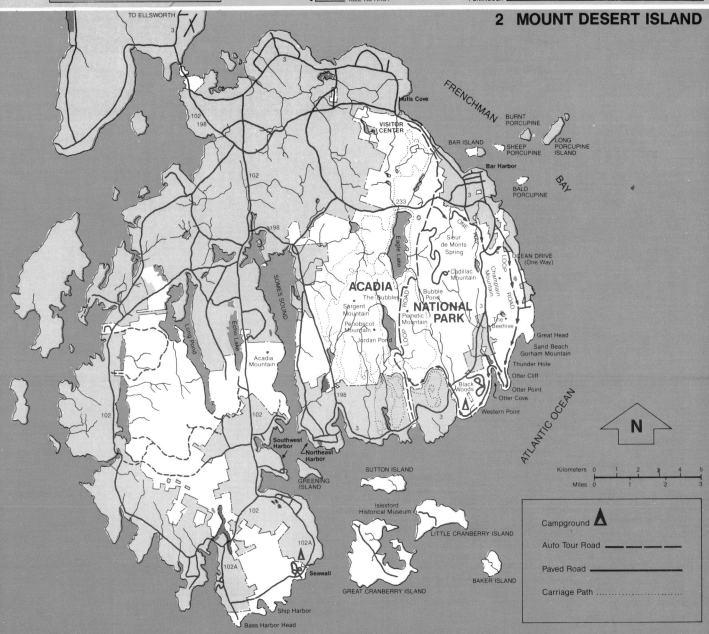

2 MOUNT DESERT ISLAND

Campground ⛺
Auto Tour Road ------
Paved Road ———
Carriage Path ....

Islands from Mountaintops

When you visit Acadia National Park, try to imagine how it has changed in the last million years. About one million years ago, a range of mountains stood here at the edge of the land, or continent. But far to the north, an ice age began. In the last million years 20 or 30 glaciers advanced and retreated over much of North America. During the last of these advances, which began about 18,000 years ago, the ice was eight or nine thousand feet thick. Can you imagine a pile of ice as thick as a mile and a half?

This continental glacier covered the range of mountains that stood beside the sea. It scraped over the land, rounding off the mountains' peaks and gouging wide valleys.

Thousands of years passed, and the mountains sank under the weight of all that ice. The glacier melted about 13,000 years ago. The mountains had become bare granite islands with no soil for plants to grow. How, then, did Acadia change into a national park covered with hundreds of kinds of trees, shrubs, and flowers?

Mount Desert Island From Baker Island ►

Soil

On mountain hikes, you can find out how Acadia got its soil. Soil is made of sand mixed with tiny bits of decayed plants and animals.

Acadia's sand was formed by plant action and weathering. When water freezes in rock cracks, the ice makes the cracks wider. This breaks the rock into sand. Rocks are also made into sand when the pioneer plants, algae and fungi, combine to make lichens. Lichens make a weak acid that breaks down rock surfaces.

Sometimes sand washes into a dip or hollow. The hollow becomes a solution pit where decaying plants and animals mix with sand to make soil. When enough soil gathers in a solution pit, plants begin to grow in it. Mosses and ferns grow and die and grow, adding to the soil. This is called succession, and succession goes on as grasses and flowers start to grow. Shrubs and trees follow in the succession, and they add to the soil.

In Acadia National Park, the soil changes from place to place. Here and there soil collects, mixes with decayed things, and gets deep and rich. In other areas the soil is thin because much of it blows or washes away.

New Plants Grow Where Soil Has Formed

Small Plants Cling To Thin Soil—Great Head

Gifts from the Soil

Because soil has formed on Mt. Desert Island, we receive the gift of plants. But they must adapt to different kinds of soil and many kinds of weather.

Some plants grow in thin, sandy soil. They could never grow in a bog where the soil is soggy with water. But the pitcher plant and round-leaf sundew adapt well in a bog because swarms of insects supply some of their food. The pitcher plant's flower and fruit stand tall on a thin stem. Its leaves, shaped like big cream pitchers, grow near the ground and hold water. Insects drown in this water, and the leaf gives off a juice that digests their soft parts.

Look very low on the ground of a bog to find the tiny plant called round-leaf sundew. Each sundew leaf is covered with sweet sticky hairs. Insects are attracted to the leaves but soon find themselves stuck in the gooey hairs. When an insect struggles to get away, the leaf hairs bend over and trap it. Then the insect dies, and the hairs give off a juice that digests it. Would you say the sundew has its stomach on the outside?

Pitcher Plant Blossom

Pitcher Plant Leaf

Round-Leaf Sundew

Mountain Flowers

On a walk up the mountainside, hikers with sharp eyes can spot changes in the soil. At the base of the mountain, the ground is soft and springy. Spruce and balsam fir trees grow in an acid soil covered with needles and leaves. Because of the acid soil, needles and leaves decay more slowly, so they form a thick cushion. When this cushion decays, it forms a rich part of the soil called *humus* or *duff*.

During July, in sunnier parts of the forest, the ground is splashed with bright red berries of bunchberry dogwood. In damp soil, the shrub meadowsweet reaches its white or pink blossoms to the sun.

High up the mountain, the soil is thinner and fewer trees grow. In some places the soil has been washed off the granite rocks. But here and there, an American harebell finds a bit of soil between boulders. It pushes its blue bell out for you to see, but not to pick. You'll want to leave the many flowers you see for others to enjoy. Besides, they will only wilt and die sooner if you carry them away.

Near the top, if you look very carefully in protected hollows, you may find the blooms of bright red wood lilies swaying on tall stems.

Bunchberry Dogwood

Meadowsweet

Wood Lily—Great Head Summit

A New Forest

Hiking up these mountains, you'll see changes in the trees. Near the ocean, white spruce grow in spite of the drying effects of wind and salt spray. Up from the shore, red spruce and fir trees grow in thicker, wetter soil.

High on the mountains, the warm growing season is short. Cold winds dry the soil and plants. Pitch pines hold their cones until they're ripe enough to drop their seeds. The wind turns some of these trees into flag trees with branches growing to one side.

In October of 1947, a strong wind whipped a fire out of a burning peat bog into the forest. The fire traveled ten miles in two hours. After the fire, over 17,000 acres of trees had turned to black skeletons.

Since that time, a succession of plants has created a new forest. First to grow were low shrubs and the broadleaf trees — aspen, maple, and birch. Years later, small evergreens such as pines, firs, and spruces sprang up in the shade of the broadleaf trees. Unless other things like fire, wind, or beaver activity disrupt the forest, these evergreens tend to grow tall and crowd out the aspens and others. A new evergreen forest will have grown in the ashes of the old one.

Flag Trees—Acadia Mountain

Two Years of Cones—Pitch Pine

Birch Trees Grow First—Great Head

Early People

The first people to enjoy the place now known as Acadia were the Indians who lived year-round along the coast of Maine and on some of the bigger islands. In birch bark canoes, they traveled on the rivers and around Mount Desert Island.

The Indians fished and dug clams to eat. Their campsites are marked by heaps of clam shells. Hundreds and thousands of years later, scientists dug into these shell heaps. They found tools made of bone and stone and baskets made of grasses and birch bark. You can see many of these artifacts in the Abbe Museum at Sieur de Monts Spring. This is a spring where Indians got their fresh water and where George Dorr, the first Acadia National Park Superintendent, built a springhouse. Nearby at the Nature Center, you can taste the clear, cool water that bubbles up where Indians once drank.

Today Sieur de Monts also has a nature display called the Wild Gardens. Here the Bar Harbor Garden Club has gathered many of Acadia's native plants from beach, bog, and mountain. It's a good place to learn about the plants you've wondered about as you hiked all over the island.

Stone Tools—Abbe Museum Of Stone Age Antiquities

Artifacts—Grass And Birch Bark

Springhouse—Sieur De Monts Spring

Settlers

In the 1600s, Europeans explored this newly discovered land. One of them was the French explorer, Champlain. As he sailed by, he saw an island with bare and rocky mountain tops, which he named *L'isle des Monts Deserts*, French for *The Island of Bare Mountains.*

Champlain claimed the island for the King of France, along with much of eastern Canada and the coast land as far south as New Jersey. But in 1606, the English claimed the same land for the Colony of Massachusetts. For about 150 years, France and England fought over Acadia or traded it back and forth. In 1775, it was held by the English, so after the American Revolution, it became part of the U.S.

Settlers soon followed. They earned a living by lumbering, fishing, boat building, and quarrying granite. Even today fishing and boat building are important to people on the western side of Mount Desert Island.

You can explore more of this story if you take a boat cruise to visit the Islesford Historical Museum on Little Cranberry Island. Here you'll see the spinning wheel, model boats, books, tools, and other things brought here by early settlers.

Islesford Historical Museum—Little Cranberry Island

Baker Island

On a historic cruise to Baker Island, you can feel how it was to settle an island. The cruise starts on a ferry from Northeast Harbor. At Baker Island, you are rowed ashore in a rocking boat called a dory. Once you're on the island, a park naturalist tells how William and Hanna Gilley came here in 1806. They came all the way from the mainland in a dory. Packed into the tiny boat were their three children, some animals, tools, and household goods.

The forest and the ocean shaped their world as they farmed, fished, and hunted. They cleared the land and built a home with spruce trees. Hanna spun flax to make linen for clothes, and an older son made shoes for the family.

Hanna had nine more children and taught all 12 of them in the island's school. When a lighthouse was built there, William earned $350 a year keeping the oil lamps burning. The lighthouse was a welcome sight for fishing ships returning home.

As you dory to the ferry for the ride back, you may wish you could stay longer to search the tide pools and listen to the waves lapping the shore.

Dory To Baker Island From The Ferry

Baker Island Lighthouse

Gifts from the Sea -Lobsters

At Acadia National Park, you hear a lot about the American lobster. This sea animal has its bones, or skeleton, on the outside. A lobster's claws are like two different kinds of pliers. One claw grabs, the other crushes.

Lobsters are scavengers and cannibals. They eat almost anything, even smaller or weaker lobsters.

Depending on its size, a female lobster carries between 3,000 and 75,000 fertilized eggs under her tail for nine or ten months. When she frees the eggs, they hatch into lobsters no bigger than mosquitoes. They float near the top of the water for 10 to 30 days. Many are eaten by fish, birds, and other predators. Fewer than one in 1000 of these tiny floating lobsters survive to settle on the rocky bottom of the ocean to live.

As a lobster grows, its skeleton gets too tight, so it molts, or sheds its skeleton. After 80 days and molting many times, a lobster is still only about an inch long. When it's old enough to mate at five to eight years, a lobster is over 10 inches long.

At about six years of age, a female lobster frees her first fertilized eggs. After that she produces eggs every other year.

American Lobster

Lobstering

Early settlers found many big lobsters crawling in shallows along the shore. They used them as cheap food for their servants or plowed lobsters and seaweed into the soil for fertilizer.

Today most people think lobster is a fine seafood. That's why you see so many brightly-colored buoys floating on the waters around Acadia National Park. The buoys are tied by long ropes to wooden traps sitting on the rocky sea bottom. A lobster crawls into the trap to get the bait of smelly old fish. Usually, the lobster cannot get out.

When a lobsterman checks his traps, he throws back any lobsters that are too big or too small and keeps those he can sell.

If a lobsterman finds a female with eggs, he's supposed to put a notch in her tail and put her back in the water. If another person traps that female after she has freed her eggs, the notch tells him she must be returned to the sea. Her next batch of eggs will help to keep these waters supplied with more lobsters.

Most lobstermen follow these rules. But many biologists say the rules aren't strict enough to protect the lobsters. They fear that the supply of lobsters will dwindle too much to support commercial lobstering.

Lobster Trap Buoys

Lobster Traps, Or Pots

Lobster Boat

Gifts from People

In about 1880, people of the eastern states began to vacation along the coast of Maine. Many built summer cottages on Mount Desert Island, some surrounded by a great deal of land.

People who loved the beauty of this island were afraid it might soon be covered with houses and hotels. They formed a group, bought up as much land as they could, and saved it for public use. The area became a National Monument in 1916. Then in 1919, it became the first National Park east of the Mississippi River.

After the 1947 fire, most people did not rebuild their summer homes, but gave their land to the park. That's why you can now roam through about 38,000 acres of mountains, forests, lakes, and seashore. You'll find 51 miles of carriage roads set aside for bicycling, horseback riding, and hiking. Over 120 miles of marked trails take you over mountains and shores.

In summer months you can join in star watches on Cadillac Mountain or a walk to view Life Between the Tides. A special walk for children is called Nature's Way. The park newspaper, *ACADIA'S BEAVER LOG* lists many other excellent programs guided by Park Naturalists.

Acadia National Park—A Gift From People To People

Making the Most of Your Stay

There's much to see and do at Acadia. To make the most of your stay, go to the Visitor Center with your family and plan. Here you can get a map and the park newspaper which includes a schedule of things to do.

You can see a fine, 15-minute film about the park. Then your family may decide to take a drive on the 27-mile Park Loop Road. Along this road are many places to park and look. Easy walks take you to Sand Beach, Thunder Hole, and Otter Point. Sometimes, when a wave rolls into Thunder Hole, it traps air and compresses it. Then the air bursts out and makes a big splash and a loud boom. This only happens during stormy weather.

You can hike on your own or join any of the guided mountain hikes. Good hiking shoes and things like cameras, sketching tools, or binoculars, make the park more fun.

If you are between 7 and 12 years old, see page 32. It will tell you how you can be a Junior Ranger.

All park activities are free except boat cruises and horseback rides. People in the Visitor Center will tell you how to sign up and pay for these.

In Summer, Thunder Hole Is Pretty Quiet

In Stormy Weather, Thunder Hole Thunders

Be a Junior Ranger

In four steps, you can become a Junior Ranger. Step one is to get a Junior Ranger Kit during work hours from the Visitor Center, Sieur de Monts Nature Center, or afternoons only at Blackwoods and Seawall Campground entrance stations.

For step two, you choose two Naturalist Programs to go on and have the leader of these sign the forms in the kit. Will you choose to learn about Acadia's trees by studying Bark, Leaves and Needles or join an early evening Beaver Watch? Maybe you'll go on the Nature's Way Walk for Children. Each one is different. One ranger might have you take a hike on which a partner leads you blindfolded on a short trail where you will touch, feel, and smell things along the way. Then you go back along the trail without your blindfold.

On another walk, the ranger may talk about a period thousands of years ago when glaciers covered this part of the country. Then you'll find out why a big boulder is balanced on top of Bubble Mountain.

Naturalists know you'll make new discoveries every time you join them on a walk through Acadia.

Boulder Balances Atop Bubble Mountain

Will You Learn About Lakes?

Have The Ranger Sign The Form In Your Kit

Discovery Hunts
-Creature Features

The third step in becoming a Junior Ranger is to do some activities on your own. These are suggested in your kit.

They include a crossword puzzle about Acadia and a word jumble about the animals in the park. There are things to draw and write about.

A discovery hunt sends you looking for things that are older than you, things that move, and food for an insect. It says find "something that is always breaking but never broken." Of course, you don't collect these but just list and tell about them.

If you choose the Creature Feature, you'll visit a tidepool and learn about life between high tide and low tide. This is a time to be very careful because of the slippery rocks. After you explore the tidepool you get to design a never-before-seen animal that might survive in a tidepool. You can build a model of your animal or draw it. Sounds like fun!

When you have done the required number of activities, you will receive an award to show that you are an official Junior Ranger at Acadia National Park. You'll even be famous enough to have your name posted on bulletin boards at the Visitor Center and campgrounds.

Daisies — Food For An Insect?

Do A Special Project

Study A Relief Map

Win An Award And Be Famous!

The Tide Pool World

During high tide, water covers a whole world that lives among the rocks along the shore. At low tide, you can explore this watery world when you go on a tide pool walk with a park naturalist. The naturalist shows you many kinds of sea life, and then you can hunt for them in the tide pools.

As you walk carefully over the slippery seaweed, you may find a dog whelk. This is a snail that lives mostly in water, feeding on tiny animals.

If you find a crab, be sure to hold it from the back, so it can't pinch you.

Starfish eat other animals, even the mussel, locked tight in its two shells. The starfish pushes its stomach into the mussel and digests it right in the shell.

But starfish have enemies too; crabs and sea gulls. If an enemy grabs one of its arms, or rays, the starfish can let go of the ray. That's how a five-pointed star turns into a four-pointed one. But this lucky animal can grow a new ray where the old one dropped off.

All of these animals can only live in the very cold waters of Acadia. So, of course, you put them back in the water after you've had a good look.

Tide Pool Walk

Dog Whelk

Rock Crab

Starfish, Big And Little

Birds

There are many kinds of birds that live in or visit Acadia. With binoculars on an early morning walk, you might see a red crossbill, cedar waxwing, or any of over 300 kinds of birds.

Along the shore you find double-crested cormorants swimming or you may see these big black birds flying low over the bay. They dive for fish and stay under water for a long time, chasing their dinner. Later, they perch on rocks and spread their wings to dry.

Four kinds of gulls regularly fly around Acadia. The smallest, with a black head, is the laughing gull. The largest is the great black-backed gull. The most common is the herring gull. Bonaparte's gull is the fourth. Since gulls are scavengers, one may swoop down to clean up your picnic.

During a cruise, you often see one or two of these scavengers flying over the boat. You always see them flocking around lobster boats. They want to eat the old bait the lobstermen throw out each time they empty a trap. Gulls make good cleanup crews.

Double-Crested Cormorants

Herring Gull

Other Animals

Many other animals live in Acadia, but they're not as easy to see. Most animals protect themselves by hiding or going out only at night.

Beavers are busy at dawn and dusk. In summer, you may want to sit beside an active beaver lodge about two hours before dusk. Be quiet and you may see a beaver as it swims to the edge of a pond to cut aspen or birch trees to add to its lodge or dam. In the fall, beavers store tree branches and twigs under the water for a winter supply of food.

From the top of Cadillac Mountain, you can look down at the valley below and see the dams of lodges of these hard workers.

You must be out very early in the morning to spot the snowshoe or varying hare. Its big feet give this animal one of its names. Because its feet are big like snowshoes, it can walk across the snow without sinking in too deep.

This cousin of the rabbit is also called a varying hare because the color of its coat changes, or *varies*. In summer, a brown coat helps the hare hide among plants. As fall turns to winter, the hare sheds its brown fur and grows a white coat so its enemies cannot see it against the snow-covered ground.

Snowshoe Hare In Summer Coat ➤

Mountain Hikes

You find out a lot about rocks on any of the mountain hikes. On your own or with a ranger, you can start with the smallest at Sand Beach, where you pick up the sand and study its tiny grains. About one fourth of the grains are ground-up rocks. The rest are broken shells.

On a geology hike you hear how hot, molten rock, called magma, pushed up under other layered rocks. The magma cooled and became granite. Later the glacier scraped away most of the layered rock and changed the peaks into lower granite mountains.

There are other signs of the glacier's work on Acadia Mountain. From the top you look down on Somes Sound, a fjord, or basin, carved out by a glacier and filled with sea water. You see where the glacier moved along, carrying rocks and sand beneath it. Under the weight of the ice, rocks cut deep scratches, or glacial grooves in the granite. Sand beneath the glacier ground away and polished the rock, making it smooth.

Acadia Mountain is one of the few places in the park to find glacial polish and striations, or scratches. The others have weathered and eroded away from this constantly changing island.

The Fjord, Somes Sound, From Acadia Mountain

Glacial Grooves

Your
Changing Park

Acadia National Park always changes. It has grown from a national monument of 5,000 acres to a national park of over seven times that size. Will it continue to grow? Will people donate more land, or will the government have a chance to buy more? How will the park change in the future?

Fire changed Acadia when it destroyed about one third of the park's evergreen forest. Now a new forest of broadleaf trees grows in its place. They provide more habitats for more animals. But later the evergreens will grow tall again and crowd out the broadleaf trees.

Water changes Acadia all the time. Stormy winter waves lift big boulders out of the water and tumble them onto the shore. Waves carry most of the grains of Sand Beach out to sea every winter. Even after the sand washes back in spring, it is shifted about by wind and water. Thunder Hole and other strange shapes carved by water tell the story of an endless battle between land and sea.

You can be sure of one thing. You'll find a different place each time you return to Acadia National Park.

Sunset Over Great Cranberry Island ►

Other National Parks in the East

In 1919, Acadia became the first national park in the east. Then in 1940, GREAT SMOKY MOUNTAINS NATIONAL PARK was dedicated. Preserved in this park are farms of the early settlers of Tennessee and North Carolina. Nature's finest artistry paints this park with wild flowers in spring and fiery colored leaves in the autumn.

MAMMOTH CAVE NATIONAL PARK has within its boundaries the longest cave in the world. Many different tours from easy to very hard take visitors through the cave. Hikes and nature walks offer a topside view of a vast hardwood forest, wild flowers, and some animals.

EVERGLADES NATIONAL PARK is a flat-lying park, covered with sawgrass standing in water. The sawgrass plain is dotted with green humps which are hammocks, islands covered with mangrove and mahogany trees. Alligators, spiders, and colorful liguus snails live in the park. Beautiful big birds flock to this southern tip of Florida, making the Everglades a birdwatcher's dreamland.

Cable Mill—Great Smoky Mountains National Park

Lantern Tour—Mammoth Cave National Park

Egrets—Mrazek Pond—Everglades National Park

The Author and Illustrators

Wyoming-born Ruth Radlauer's love affair with national parks began in Yellowstone. During her younger years, she spent her summers in the Bighorn Mountains, in Yellowstone, or on Casper Mountain.

Ed and Ruth Radlauer, graduates of the University of California at Los Angeles, are authors of many books for young people. Along with their young adult daughter and sons, they photograph and write about a wide variety of subjects ranging from motorcycles to monkeys.

The Radlauers live in California, where Ruth and Ed spend most of their time in the mountains near Los Angeles.